From Little Pauper Girl to *"Princess-Bride"* for Ever After

Joyce (Grammer) Lacey

RWG Publishing
PO Box 596
Litchfield, IL 62056
https://rwgpublishing.com/

Published in the United States of America

Dedicated to My Children and Grandchildren

Todd, Jill, Trent, and Grandchildren and Great-Grandchildren: Shane, Preston, Peyton and Vivian, Also Shane's Wife Amber and their children, Jadon and Caleb and Noah.

I wanted you to know a little about your ancestors. I do not have much history to pass on from my grandparents because I did not meet either of my grandparents on my Fathers side, and only my grandfather on my mother's side. I was about thirteen when I met Grandpa Nicholson. In my story, I tell about my visit with him.

I am eighty-two this April, 2020, so I do have quite a history to relate to you just because of the length of my life.

I also dedicate this memoir to you the reader

I wrote this memoir not just for my family but to anyone who would want to know about how God can impact a life such as mine and how He can impact yours.

I believe that there is much in my story that will inform, encourage and up-lift anyone who reads it. They will be able to see what God's overall plan is for humanity and how everyone in one way or the other is striving for the same thing.

Acknowledgements

I want first of all to thank my wonderfully patient husband who allowed me to take the time I needed to write the story of my life.

I also want to thank all the remarkable friends that are mentioned in my story. They have helped shape my life and gave me the confidence and support I needed to live, love, laugh and be happy. They also helped me to stay strong in my faith and they were instrumental in encouraging and uplifting me when I felt as if I were falling or failing.

My friends at the Writer's Gallery: Leader: Andrew Irvin, Joyce M., Eric, Ron, Judith, April, Carol, Ezekiel, Kathy, Debbie, and Virginia and Mike. I cannot thank you enough for your encouragement and sometimes tough critiques that humbled me and helped me to write from the reader's point of view. Your assistance gave me the determination to continue writing. Thank You.

I also want to thank my new neighbor Irmgart who has helped me so much with my lack of computer skills.

Above all I want to thank You Heavenly Father for giving me the inspiration to write about You and Your plan for all mankind through my life experiences. And it is my fervent prayer that this story will glorify You.

And thank You Jesus, You were always present to love, up-lift and encourage me.

And I am so grateful to You Holy Spirit, for helping and guiding me with the ability to actually write down the words that needed to be said.

Forward

God has had His hand on Joyce's life from birth to this day. Everyone who meets and/or talks with her sees the joy she has both for the Lord and for people.

Her laugh and smile are infective and she will lift your spirit to new heights. She knows and understands the love of God, Jesus, and the Holy Spirit.

I know that you will enjoy and better understand the Trinity after reading her writings.

I'm most blessed for you see, I am her husband.

Larry Lacey

Table of Contents

Introduction

Everyone loves a mystery. So, I think that is why God uses mysteries to draw us into His word. I just solved a "God mystery" while writing my memoir.

There is a thread that runs through my entire life and runs through yours too, if you are a child of God.

Clue: There is a theme, I challenge you to find it and solve the "God Mystery."

Joyce (Grammer) Lacey

Grammer Family in 1943

Daddy, (Frank Grammer) Sister,(Elaine) Me, (Joyce) Momma (Blanche)

From Little Pauper Girl to "Princess-Bride" For Ever After

Chapter 1

Give Me Five!

(Years from 1938-1943)

O ne day as I was reflecting on the first five years of my life, I thought to myself, 'Was I rich or was I poor?' I had to really think about that. Here is my story.

My life began as a country girl. I was born April 19th, 1938, in Prairie Grove, Arkansas at the Elizabeth Hospital. Therefore, my name: Joyce "Elizabeth" Grammer. Though the hospital was in Prairie Grove, we lived in a share crop house in Mountain Grove, Arkansas.

Elaine and me in front of our Share Crop House
(Mountain Grove, Arkansas, 1940)

Elaine age 7, Me age 2 with our Dog Brownie

Daddy was silly serious, I know that sounds like an oxy-moron but by that I mean he was comical, told funny stories and sang silly songs and generally kept us all laughing and yet he was very strict. It was extremely important to him that we, my sister Elaine and I, learned to be obedient. We were never to talk back for *any* reason.

My Father, George, William, Franklin, (Frank) Grammer, loved the Lord and wrote gospel music. He published his songs and other song writers work in "Favorite Songs of the Church" that he compiled.

2

He received a doctor's degree in music, however we moved to California before his diploma was to come in the mail. It was damaged when it finally did arrive. Daddy sent it back and asked for another copy but one never came. Therefore, he would not go by, Doctor Grammer.

I found a partial article written in an old newspaper about Daddy it said he, *"joined the staff at the Martin Davis Co. and served in the capacity as song writer, teacher, and evangelistic singer. He has written hundreds of songs and is editor and compiler of many song books, served as president of the Eureka Normal School of Music, (now Vice President).* It also said, *"Frank Grammer is one of the best-informed men musically. He was at one-time President of FA Music Company and a chartered school of music."* The rest of the article was missing so I don't know what else it said about him but I did want this to be in my memoir to honor him.

The master's degree diploma he received from Eureka School of Music in Mena; Arkansas is beautiful. It is larger than one might think a diploma would be. It measures 21x17 inches. Daddy and Mama framed it in a lovely, antique frame of decorative wood and I have it hanging on my wall and am honored to have inherited it.

At church, Daddy led the singing during worship. He would now be referred to as a Music Minister. He was the actual minister much of the time. He loved to speak so he would preach anytime he was needed.

My mother, Blanche, Leona, Nicholson, was a quiet, soft-spoken, pleasant lady.

3

She was always ready to listen and help with anything we needed. She was a great cook and excellent seamstress. She made most all our clothes and drew the patterns herself. I'm sure Mama could have been a famous dress designer had she lived in the right era, time and place. She made short sets for us to wear in the summer and our dresses were made from flour sacks that came in pretty prints. I did receive a store-bought dress for my second birthday from my half brother Jesse who lived in California. When Mama put it on me, I felt pretty as a princess.

Me showing my store bought dress my brother Jesse sent me on my birthday
Age 2

My sister, Elaine, who was five years older than me, treated me like I was *her* baby. As we walked along with our family on our way to church, she would carry me piggy-back. I remember singing and

4

looking at the pretty little yellow, blue and white wildflowers along the path. I can still feel my arms around Elaine's neck and her hands supporting my bottom. Sundays were a big day for our family. After church we usually had dinner on the grounds or at someone's house. We sang and played and enjoyed the fellowship all day. We ended the day going back to worship the Lord at our quaint little church.

Daddy was also a farmer. Our small farm had chickens, a pig, a dog, a cat, and a cow with a new born calf. I don't remember the calf's birth. My parents sheltered my sister and me from, "such things." I have a very sweet memory of the little calf laying its head on my lap. Elaine and I would just sit down on the ground and the calf would come and lay down beside us. We could put its head on our lap so that we could pet it.

When Daddy milked the cow, he would tell me to open my mouth and he'd spray milk into it. Our cat (whose whiskers I once cut off) also got a treat of warm milk right from the cow. Mama told me that a cat's whiskers helped them to get around in the dark at night. I felt very sad and vowed never to do that again. Soon after that however, I cut my own bangs. I got a spanking that time. From then on, I paid attention to my parent's rules that, "Scissors are off limits!"

Daddy always planted a garden, so we had fresh vegetables when they were in season. Mama canned fruits and vegetables and put them in the storm shelter to keep them cool and to save for food during the winter. Since I was only three, my memory is a little bit sketchy as to when and where things happened.

To the best of my recollection, there were times food was scarce. Sometimes during the winter, all we had was milk, eggs, biscuits and gravy, and butter that we churned. I was told I was a. "big helper" when churning butter. I remember going up on my tip toes and pulling up on the handle of the churn and then pushing it back down. As I was "helping" churn one time, a wasp flew into my mouth and I bit it in two. Thankfully, wasps don't fly backwards, that could have been quite disastrous!

Sometimes while sitting on momma's lap she would dip her biscuit into her coffee and let me have a bite. So, obviously, we had coffee.

Though we didn't have much money, I never felt poor because our family always dressed well and mother styled our hair, by braiding or making Shirley Temple curls, using rags as curlers. She even put ribbons in our hair just to go out to play. My sister and I had so much fun together. Sometimes in Arkansas, we played outside in the warm rain, dressed only in our underpants. We had a rain barrel that collected water for bathing and washing our hair and we liked to watch it get full enough for our family to use.

A fun memory I have is when Daddy took Elaine and me to a bamboo forest. The bamboo looked as high as the sky to me. Daddy broke off a piece of bamboo and made whistles for us. I was so excited. We loved blowing our whistles. Elaine said we were pretending to be the Pied Piper, though I didn't know what that meant.

Our family bought a new house in Huntsville, Arkansas. At our new home we no longer had a farm but we still had a few chickens and a small garden. It was Elaine's and my job to exchange eggs for milk with Mrs. Johnson. It seemed a long way up a hill to where she lived. One time as we were walking to her house, we saw a black snake in the ditch by the side of the road. We ran as fast as we could. My sister was really terrified because when we lived in Mountain Grove she had been bitten by a rattlesnake. It was early one evening, as our family walked to a friend's house. There were only paths to walk on in the area where we lived and a snake was curled up in the bushes and struck Elaine's leg as we walked by. Daddy was carrying me on his shoulders. Back then people could not race off to the hospital in an emergency.

Daddy and Mama hurried to the friend's house and they put coal oil on the bite and everyone prayed. Elaine's leg drew up and it took a while to straighten out, but God healed her completely.

Mama's son Jesse was from her first marriage. Her first husband died with typhoid fever when she was eight months pregnant with Jesse. I had never met my half-brother because he married and moved to California before I was born.

We were unable to keep our new home due to the "Great Depression."

Jesse had been begging us to come to California and stay with him and his family until we could get settled. So, Mama and Daddy decided to take Jesse up on his offer.

7

I was three when the day came to move to California. I don't remember much about our stay with Jesse and his wife Georgia except for the rabbits that they raised. I know we ate lots of fried rabbit. I loved sitting on Georgia's lap as she scratched my back.

Once my sister Elaine, Jerry, Jesse's son and I went exploring at a building site. I'm sure we weren't supposed to be there but while scrounging around, we found some metal slugs that looked like coins. We thought it would be fun to use them as play money.

Their family had a Cocker Spaniel dog named Sandy. All I remember about Sandy was that he ran off several times. I do remember while we were staying at Jesse's, I met my daddy's sister, Aunt Bessie and her husband Frank. They lived in Torrance, California. On Halloween Georgia, Jesse's wife made me a ghost costume. I'm sure someone in the family called my aunt to let her know we were coming though no one told me.

They just told me that we were going to Aunt Bessie's for trick or treat. I don't think I really understood what Halloween was all about since I was only three years old.

Daddy and Mama had me go to the door by myself and I was told to say, "Trick or Treat." When Aunt Bessie opened the door and saw me, she said to her husband, "Oh No! There is a ghost out here Frank!" She went on and on until my family came up and we went in for a visit. I giggled and giggled thinking how much fun it was to think that my aunt didn't know me, that I had fooled her.

I think I was four when we left Jesse's and moved into a duplex on Truslow Street in Fullerton, California. I know I wasn't five yet.

8

Our family moved behind the Scratton's. They had a daughter named Jean who was my sister's age. Elaine and Jean became best friends.

My family moved again, about a year or so later, to an apartment, still in Fullerton on Commonwealth Ave. and across the street from Amerage Park. Since our apartment had no yard the park became our play area. There were swings, monkey bars, parallel bars, a tether-ball, croquet, ping pong, wading pool, a little shop to paint ceramics, a fish pond, so much grass to run and play on and trees to climb. The park officials allowed us to go into the ball-park free to see the donkey baseball games, the girl's softball team, and the 20/30 Club baseball team.

(Fig. 4) Elaine and me sitting on a bench at Amerage Park playing.

A lady asked us if she could take our picture that she noticed how nice we always looked when we came to the park to play. When she developed the pictures she gave us a copy.

At the end of the summer the park had a huge watermelon feed, and a barbeque for the community. That is one of my most fond memories.

Our apartment was what some people refer to as a "Shotgun House." It has been said that the name came from the fact that you could take a gun aim it through the front door and the bullet would go straight through the house and out the back door without hitting anything. Our apartment was like that. It was built in a straight line, front room, dining room, then a dividing wall right down the middle, the kitchen on one side of it and a small dressing room and bathroom on the opposite side. The back room had Mom and Dad's bed on one side and a laundry room on the other side divided only by a curtain. The front door, lined up with the back door making it possible to shoot right through it.

There was an extra mattress on Mom and Dad's bed. When people came to visit or needed a place to stay my parents would take the extra mattress off their bed, and carry it through the kitchen, to the dining room. They moved the dining table over against the buffet. The mattress just barely fit on the floor. The next morning, they picked the mattress up, put it back on Mom and Dad's bed, then they moved the dining table back to the center of the room. This happened often as we had many people stay with us, including my brother Jesse when he and his wife Georgia divorced. Another time my aunt came and stayed with us for a while so this ritual seemed normal to me.

When Evangelist Rue Porter came to town to hold a gospel meeting for our congregation, he also stayed with us. He and my father were long-time friends. They traveled all over the country together. He preached and Daddy held a music school for any members who wanted to learn a little about how to read music.

The back door of our apartment had a stairway leading down to the back yard.

The yard was just big enough for us and the other people who lived in the apartments to burn their trash in the incinerator. Burning our trash was Elaine's and my job. While burning we would pick and eat the delicious black berries that grew through the fence from the neighbor's yard behind us.

In our neighborhood there were all kinds of wonderful fruits trees like, apple, pomegranate, persimmon, and right outside our apartment next to our porch was an orange tree. We lived upstairs so the tree hung over our porch right at picking level.

Our next-door neighbor had a big home and yard and in it she had a loquat tree and that was my very favorite fruit to pick and enjoy. She also had concord grapes that we were welcome to eat. The neighbors said to help ourselves to anything in their yard that we wanted to pick and eat while we were playing. We certainly got our daily requirement of fruit.

Looking back at my first five years I can now answer my initial question at the beginning of this chapter. *Was I rich or was I poor?*

With a loving family, an enormous park for a play yard, and a neighborhood of friends who freely provided fresh fruit while we played. I realized if I had been born a "princess" and lived in a castle

I could not have been more richly blessed, than I was the first five years of my life.

Chapter 2

Unpredictable, Unimaginable Years

(1944-1949

These were WWII years. It was sometimes very scary. There were sirens that warned us, when there was an air-raid. We were to lie on or under our beds and turn out all the lights until the siren stopped. One night during an air-raid, there was a knock on our door I was so frightened. Daddy went to the door and there were two German soldiers. They said they were looking for someone and my dad told them they did not live here. Because our apartment was old, we believed they thought it to be abandoned and they could use it to stay the night. I don't remember if Daddy reported the incident or not.

Daddy planted a, "Victory Garden" as it was called during the war. Most everyone had one as the food was in short supply. I loved to go and pull up a carrot or pick a tomato to eat as I played.

I remember the day the war was over everyone was celebrating. We had been stomping on cans to donate for the war effort and when we stomped on them, they cupped around our shoes and we could walk on them. That day we walked around in them singing and shouting, "Yea! The war is over; The war is over!

***

Daddy had a heart problem and had been in the hospital. When he came home, he needed to be in a hospital bed. I stayed with him because I was too young to go to school and mom had to go to work. He told mom I was, *"a good little nurse."* I would bring him a drink of water or anything I could to help him. When He was sleeping, I remember being very quiet coloring or playing with my paper dolls. As he was recovering, He and I would walk to the post office stopping on the way to have a piece of cherry pie at the gas station. Many times, he would bring an apple to eat on our way home. We would sit down at the lumber yard and he would peel that apple all the way around without stopping. Then he would cut me a slice and then he would take a slice. I relish those special times with my Daddy.

Beginning first grade, I was so happy to see that my kindergarten teacher was also my first-grade teacher. Her name was Joyce same as mine, and I loved her. She was young and so much fun that I liked going to school. My second-grade year began a series of very difficult events in my life.

I often block out these years because they are probably the most unpleasant of all.

I began having terrible stomach pains. I had fought them for several years but they were getting consistently worse. When my parents would take me to the doctor, he would just say I had an upset stomach from something I had eaten. He would give me something to settle it. I was seven, and I became very sick. I had a fever that was getting higher and higher. My stomach pains kept getting worse and my mouth was dry and parched. I had such a high fever I

14

couldn't find a comfortable cool spot on the bed. My parents took me to the doctor and he rushed me to the hospital.

After taking x-rays doctors discovered my intestines were swollen and tight causing me to have blocked bowels. My hands started drawing up until my fingers were curled as I was very dehydrated. The only answer was to operate.

I was told the doctors were concerned because they had no experience with a problem of this kind. However, there was a doctor from New York at the hospital who was familiar with this type of surgery. Thanks to God's grace and mercy, the visiting doctor did the operation.

My parents and many other friends from church were praying and I know God answered their prayers by sending that doctor at just the right time. I almost did not come out of the surgery. The doctors said that they had given me too much ether. While in that state, I had a near-death experience.

I didn't think much about it until I was older and I read the book, "Life after Life." My vision was so similar to the people in that book that I realized I had had a, "near-death" experience.

While under the influence of the anesthetic I saw a swirling tunnel pulling me lightning fast toward something like a door with light all around it and I realized I was dying. I knew if I slipped under that door I would be gone forever from this life. I remember fighting not to go under the door, and then I woke up and the nurse was giving me oxygen and my dad was praying at my bedside.

15

I recovered well but since my immune system was so weak, I got every childhood disease imaginable that year: chicken pox, measles, mumps, whooping cough accompanied by pneumonia.

My second-grade school teacher told my mother that I didn't have enough grades for her to pass me on to the third grade but that she was going to because she thought I would do fine. I did and I was glad she passed me as I would have been very embarrassed if I had "flunked" the common expression for being held back a grade. I did struggle with math, and still do, because I missed the basics.

During my seventh year, I also experienced extreme disappointment in our family. I mentioned in the previous chapter my half-brother Jesse. He divorced his wife Georgia.

Though a child, having my brother divorce was traumatic for me. I don't think people realize how their lives involve and affect others, especially family. I was heartbroken because I loved Georgia dearly. She was so kind and warm and loving. Jesse and his son Jerry moved in with us. Remember the bed situation in our home? They stayed with us until the custody battle was over. Georgia got custody of Jerry and Jesse moved out.

My fourth and fifth grades were uneventful except my fifth-grade teacher hurt my feelings. I could not see the board and instead of telling her there was a glare on the board and I could not see the questions, when she asked me what number (1) on the board was, I just said. "I don't know."

Then the teacher said, "Well then what is number (2)"?

Again, I said, "I don't know."

Then she yelled at me, "Well what *do* you know, Joyce!?" She then went on to someone else.

I always walked home and I cried all the way to my house. When I got there momma said, "What's the matter Joyce?"

I said, "My teacher yelled at me and said, "what *do* I know?"

I think my mom straightened it all out with my teacher because she never talked like that to me again.

The traumas of those years were not over yet. I was ten when my sister Elaine woke up in extreme stomach pain. We rushed her to the emergency room as her fever was very high and something needed to be done soon. When we got to the hospital, she was writhing in pain with appendicitis. Our family doctor was out of town and they tried to wait for him to come and do the surgery. They waited so long that her appendix burst. She almost died. Again, God intervened on her behalf.

Many years later Elaine and I were discussing the book "Life after Life" and she said she also had a near-death experience. Hers was that she actually got to a place were she was next to a river. Across on the other side was our Aunt Ida who she was named after. My sister's name was "Ida" Elaine. Elaine excited about crossing over the river but Aunt Ida said, "No, Elaine, you need to go back as your family needs you now."

In April of that year I turned eleven. Elaine had recovered from her surgery and gave me a birthday party. Our parties were always fun since we lived across from the park. I opened my gifts before we went to the park. I had begun to physically develop and my sister bought me a bra. That would have been fine except one of my girlfriends had a twin brother and what did she do but go home and tell her family. Of course, the next day at school her brother told all the boys. They would come by me saying, in a sing-song-y way, "We know what you got for your birthday!" I was so humiliated I wanted to cry but I didn't.

The following July proved how true Aunt Ida's statement was to Elaine because the next unimaginable thing happened in our family.

At the annual Arkansas Picnic on the Fourth of July at the park, Daddy planned to introduce the second gospel song book that he recently finished compiling and publishing.

He planned to sing some songs from his book with my sister and her friend June and June's dad Lee Pennington. A stage was set up in the middle of the ball field for the entertainment. While Daddy sat on a bench waiting to sing, he had a massive heart attack. It was a shocking thing to happen before those people who were attending the concert.

My sister, sitting next to him, tried to help. She actually removed his false teeth as it seemed to her that he was choking on them. The Doctor was called, but Daddy did not survive.

My mom and I were across the street getting ready to go over to the park, when someone came anxiously saying, "Come quick, Mr. Grammer has had a heart attack."

I was eleven and Elaine had just turned sixteen in June. I was devastated over his death as I was truly a "Daddy's Girl"

At the funeral I could not even talk to anyone for awhile and I was rude to my neighbor and friend Lucille who tried to comfort me. As she came up to take my hand I readily shook it away. I did apologize many years later. She said she didn't even remember the incident. It was comforting to know Lucille had not held it against me

***

[Soon after I married in 1957, I dreamed that my husband and I were camping and that Daddy walked up to us as if he had never been gone. I was so angry with him I cried and bawled him out mercilessly. When I woke up, I realized I was angry at him for leaving us. But I knew it wasn't what he wanted to do, so I said, "Daddy I forgive you. I'm sorry I have been angry at you for so long." After that I never had any more dreams like that about him. It was amazing what that decision to forgive did for my peace of mind.]

After the funeral Jesse came to help us. We moved to Buena Park. Mom, Jesse, Elaine and me. Later mom decided we needed to be on our own so the three of us moved into an apartment in Buena Park. It was a rough town, no police, and referred to as "Bony Jungles."

Joyce (Grammer) Lacey

Chapter 3

Family Tragedies

1961-1957

I decided to write about the tragedies in our family because I believe the Lord wants me to. There are times when He wakes me up at night. When He does, I cannot go to sleep until I make a decision to do, whatever it is that He has put on my heart. I always want to please Him but I really did not want to write about the terrible things that happened in our family. However, in the Bible, God always told, "the good, the bad and the ugly," about the people that He loved, so I believe that is what He wants me to do also.

A Tragedy on My Mother's side of the Family

Though I loved my brother Jesse, even at three, I was a little afraid of him. In 1941 when we were staying in his home, he was very hard on his son Jerry. He whipped him so hard for most anything and everything. I don't know if he was ever violent with his wife Georgia.

Because of our Son Todd, I know about bi-polar problems. I am sure Jesse was tormented by that mental disorder. There were no diagnoses for the mental and emotional problems of that kind back then. Jesse had a history of violence. He fought with my dad at one time. But they had reconciled their differences before Daddy died.

He threatened my sister one time just because he was in his angry mood.

If he came in to our house whistling we knew he was having a good day and all would be fine. If, however, he came in sullen and quiet we, my sister and I, knew we had better get up and look busy working around the house or just go somewhere so we didn't have to contend with him.

Jesse also threatened me when I was fifteen. When he came to our house that day, I noticed he was not in a good mood. I stayed home from school because I was sick.

Knowing Jesse, I knew his was going to do something to me. So, I casually got up off the couch to go into another room. As I did, he got up and walked toward me. I walked a little faster and he grabbed my arm. I had a sweater on so I was able to pull my arm out and run out the back door. My mom stopped him from following me. He never ever was violent with my mom. He loved her and respected her.

We believed Jesse was jealous of Elaine and me because he had had Mom all to himself for so many years, that it was hard for him to accept mom having a second family.

I do know he loved us, but his mental condition got in the way of his ability to control his violent outbursts.

After Jesse came after me, my mom knew she had to call the authorities on him. He was picked up and restrained in the hospital for psychiatric evaluation. They did say he was, "rattled," (a far cry from Bi-polar). They just let him out. There was no help for him. The authorities did issue a restraining order to keep him from coming within a certain distance of our house. However, one night I was sitting on the couch doing homework and our dog, Danny Boy, started barking. He had a different bark when it was someone he knew. Jesse always liked Danny Boy. I looked up and the door knob was slowly turning. I jumped up and locked the door quickly. Then I heard who I was sure was Jesse, walking around to the back door. Danny Boy was on the back porch. We always kept the back door locked when we brought him in for the night. I heard Jesse talking to him quietly. That was the last time he ever came around.

He had married again but was getting a divorce from this woman too.

I do know Jesse loved us; He would brag on us to other people. He tried to be good to us and helpful. He would buy us *very* nice gifts. When we were little, he would tease, and play with us. After Daddy died, he also tried to be, "The man" in our family but his mental condition always got in the way.

The month before Larry and I married in 1957, Mom and I got a phone call from a long-time friend of Jesse's. He informed us that Jesse had shot and killed himself.

Mama said to me, "Excuse me honey," and went into the bedroom, fell on her knees and cried and cried.

I wanted to comfort her but I didn't know what to do. I was sad because I did love Jesse but all I could think of was that we were safe now and he was, hopefully, at peace too.

23

Later when I had time to think about everything, I tried to put myself in Jesse's place to understand why he would commit suicide.

He had lost his first wife and son through divorce, then the person he loved most in the entire world, Mama, seemed to turn on him by calling the police. Lastly, he was in the process of a second divorce. I could understand how he must have felt inside. In his mind he had nothing left to live for.

God does not promise anyone perfection in this life. However, He does promise, peace that passes all understanding and I have found that peace. So wished Jessie would have found that peace too.

Another Family Tragedy, Daddy's Side

Three years after we were married, Larry completed his service time in Seattle. It was 1961 when we moved to Garden Grove, California.

Aunt Bessie had a daughter named Muriel and she had a daughter named Karleen. Karleen was in her late teens during the time when I was three and we lived with Jesse in Gardena. Years later Karleen married a man who became an alcoholic.

Larry and I were excited to find out that Karleen and her husband lived on the same street in Garden Grove that we did but several miles down the road. She and her husband had four children and another one on the way. Though we lived fairly close, I hadn't been able to visit Karleen much. We hadn't lived there long and she was a busy mother and worked out of her home as a CPA.

24

One day Aunt Bessie and Uncle Frank showed up at our door horrified. Karleen's husband had gotten drunk and killed her and the baby died also. Her husband was arrested and convicted of a double murder.

It was truly one of the worst things we could have imagined to ever happen in our family. I cannot even begin to express how I felt. It was truly a nightmare but I wasn't able to wake up as it actually did happen. Her mother Muriel adopted the four children.

These scriptures have been a great comfort to me: *"I have told you these things, so that in me you may have peace. In this world you will have trouble. But take heart! I have overcome the world."* John 16: 33 (NIV) One day when Jesus comes to rule and reign, all things *will* be perfect.

Joyce (Grammer) Lacey

Chapter 4

"Bony Jungles" Days of Decision

(1950-1957)

I was apprehensive about starting the sixth grade at a new school. I had been in Fullerton all my previous school years. The thought of making new friends did frighten me a little. However, on my first day at school a girl came up to me and said, "Hi, I'm Sandra, who are you?" We became best friends. I will never forget her kindness that day. She had a horse and we had such fun. She took me riding all over the Buena Park hills. I loved Sandra and her mom, Pansy. I think my mom and Sandra's mom must have been cut out of the same mold as they were truly wonderful Christian mothers.

When I was thirteen my mom and I went to visit my grandfather in Greenville, Texas. He was in his eighties and I had never met him.

Arriving at Greenville we got out of the air-conditioned bus and a blast of heat, of about 120 degrees hit us. I said, "MOM it feels like a furnace here!"

She laughed and said, "You're in Texas now, honey." I decided right then I never wanted to live in Texas. I know now there are some very nice places in Texas, y'all, so don't get mad at me.

27

My grandfather lived with my aunt and uncle but the house belonged to him. They had a grocery store right behind the house. My uncle and aunt owned the store now but originally, it too was Grandpa's.

Grandpa was a very interesting person. I loved him immediately. He had a little geranium growing in a pot. I said, *"Grandpa, why are you growing a geranium in a pot?"*

He said, "Well how else would you grow a Geranium?"

I laughed and said; "Well they grow in bushes out in California."

He looked at me and said, "Naw, you're just kidding your old grandpa."

I tried to convince him but he wasn't buying it.

While in Texas I met many of my cousins. They took me to the movies, miniature golfing, and family members invited us over several times to eat dinner or for a barbeque.

Once when my cousins took me miniature golfing and we were on our way home in one of my cousin's cars, we were all talking and suddenly, everyone was silent.

Then one of my cousins said, in a strong Texas drawl, "Don't she tawk cute?"

We all laughed and I said, "Hey! You guys are the ones talking cute!" Then we all laughed at each other.

When Mom and I went to take the bus back to California it was out of commission. The only available bus was full of young men, right out of boot camp. Some were in the Marines and some were in the Navy. Mom and I were the only females.

Back then people dressed up when they traveled. Therefore, I had on a taffeta print dress, hat and high heels. When mom and I got on the bus all the service men spread out so that my mom and I could not sit together. Finally, after my mom made one young man feel guilty by saying, "now come on honey, let me and my daughter sit together it's going to be a long ride" so one young man said, "OK" and he gave up his seat for us. It was great fun. I had a ball singing all night long with them. We sang each of the Navy and Marine hymns and many popular, gospel, and country songs. The next day, there was a boy with beautiful blue eyes that sat right in front of me. He had a beautiful voice and he sang, "Only Make Believe" to me. I gave him my address. We wrote to each other all during his time in the service and until I was engaged to Larry. A total of about six years. I have kept his letters because they are so sweet and I figure some day my kids and grandkids might enjoy reading them.

I had so much fun in Texas but it was good to be home again and to share with my friends what I did while visiting with my family, and the unusual bus ride. I think my girlfriends would like to have been traveling with me on that bus trip home.

As I said before, Buena Park was a rough town. Many of my friends when we were in junior high started to experiment with smoking, drinking, and by eighth grade even some drugs. These kids were curious about the world and wanted to try out everything it offered. Basically, good kids, but by the time we were in the eighth grade, things were getting out of hand.

Being raised in a loving Christian home and knowing how God felt about all of those things, I did not participate. Strangely, I was not tempted, I know now that because of my upbringing, I had a desire to please God. I also read in God's word that the Holy Spirit is sent as a guide and to keep me from temptation.

However, I loved my friends and wanted to be with them so I attended parties with them. Many of these parties had no adult supervision. Alcohol was available, as the liquor cabinet, was always open to anyone who wanted to drink. Most of the kids did drink and smoke and do whatever else they wanted to do.

On one such occasion, I went to a party with some friends. The party was getting wild. Kids were dancing, drinking, and smoking, and some kids were in the bedrooms.

I felt very uncomfortable. I was in the living room next to a doorway that led into a bedroom. This *very* handsome, tall, blond, curly haired guy came in the front door. He was wearing Levis and *no shirt*. Granted it was a very hot night. He came up to me rested his arm on the doorway, over me, looked down at me and said,

"What are you doing here?"

I said, "I came with my friends."

"You don't belong here, why don't you let me take you home?"

30

Without hesitation, I said, "O.K." I would normally never go with a stranger. I told my friends that brought me to the party that I was leaving with this guy.

He took me straight home just like he promised. A funny thing is that I do not remember any conversation in the car or even giving him my address. I just recall getting in the car and then out of the car at my house and saying, "Thank you." As I walked to the door, I thought to myself, I didn't even ask his name! Turning around to hail him down, neither he nor the car, were anywhere in sight.

The next day, I asked my friends who he was and they said they didn't know, they thought he was my friend. No one ever saw him again.

One day I was meditating on the incident that happened when I was a teenager. I believe God was being a Father to me as He promised. (Psalm 68:5) I was a fatherless child in this world. Wow! sending an angel disguised as a teenage boy so not to be conspicuous. I thought of many other times He, protected me, and took care of me during the many years that followed. Psalms 34:7 says, *"The Angel of the Lord encamps around those who fear Him and He delivers them."* (NIV) Thank you, Father God.

My "Bony Jungle" friends and I started high school in Fullerton 1951-52. It was getting more and more difficult to be with my friends. I loved them and I really was in a quandary as to what to do about it. I did not want come off as," Holier than Thou," so to speak.

I had a big crush on a boy at high school. I wanted, in the worst way, for him to invite me out on a date. One day I did get a phone call from him and he said he wanted to come over to talk to me. I was so excited I just knew that he was going to ask me out on a date. Much to my surprise and disappointment, he was asking me to go out with him and *his date* on a blind date. When they came to pick me up, I saw that it was not a "blind date" at all. With him was a guy who had asked me out many times and I had continually refused to go out with him. I was not happy to say the least but I went anyway. Needless to say, I was very glad when the date was over. I made a vow never-ever to except an invitation to go on a blind date no matter who asked me to go.

When this guy came to my house to ask me out on the double date, he made this comment, "You know, Joyce, a lot of boys would like to take you out but you run around with that rough crowd from, "Bony Jungles." I was embarrassed when I heard that and made the decision right then to separate from the crowd I was hanging out with.

I know my Father in heaven impressed on my heart a way to tell my friends that would not offend them. James 1:17 reminded me that every good action… is from God. So, I got them all together at school during recess and explained my dilemma. I told them how much I liked them and how I hated not to hang out with them but I did not do any of the things they were doing and I felt uncomfortable.

I told them that they were still my friends and that they would always be.

One of my friends said, "Joyce, I would give anything to be doing what you are doing right now but it is too late for me."

I said to her, "No it's not, just hang out with me."

She said, "No, I can't. What would I do when the kids all say, 'Come on let's all go over to your house and have a party?' Then they just go to my house and my parents are usually are not home so the kids drink and can do whatever they want." I felt so sad for her when she told me that.

I remained friends with all of them and they seemed to understand and respect my decision. I never preached to them about how or what they should do but they were aware of my convictions.

I was concerned about their lives. I knew they were all headed down paths that would ultimately cause them much pain, unhappiness and grief and it did. But I am happy to report that most of them are now living good productive lives.

It was very difficult at first to eat lunch by myself and not have friends to hang out with, however, God provided a wonderful new friend, Lois, who had just moved into our area. She and her family came to the church I attended. She also went to high school with me. She and I sang duets together. A couple of boys joined us and we then sang as a quartet most every week at singing conventions held at many of the churches in the Southern California area. At the end of our sophomore year, Lois and I were walking along at school and she turned and said, "Hi, Larry."

I said, "Hey, he's cute, who is he?"

Lois said, "Oh, that's Larry Lacey. I have typing with him. He's really a nice guy, want to meet him?"

I said, "Sure! The next recess, Lois introduced me to Larry. That weekend another friend from church was having an ice-cream party at her house. Lois asked Larry if he would like to go with me. He said, "Yes." I was so excited, that after Larry left, I jumped up and down and said, "He can go, he can go!"

The ice cream party was wonderful I was very impressed with Larry. He helped crank the ice cream. He was so polite and thoughtful to everyone. I really liked him and hoped he liked me the same. I was thrilled when he asked me out again to a DeMolay beach party.

I didn't want to wear my own bathing suit to the Party. A friend of mine named Delores offered me her pink print, bathing suit with a little ruffled skirt. I tried her bathing suit on and I thought, "This is perfect!" Delores was also one of my church friends. She was a beautiful girl. I thought she looked like Kathryn Graceson in the Showboat musical of 1951. Delores married Morris Taylor, a forever friend from church.

I also met a girl at school that became one of my best friends. We had modern dance class together. We double dated often as her boyfriend was a friend of my now steady boyfriend, Larry.

Buena Park kids attended Fullerton Union High School, so I renewed my friendship with my kindergarten through fifth grade best friend Kay. Kay was a drill team leader and I was on the team. Actually, it was more of a dance team as we did dance routines and it was required that we be able to pick up dance steps and do the splits. During football half-time we were part of the band formations and we also did dances like the "Highland Fling," and we ended many routines on the field with the "Chorus Line." Kay had taught me dance steps when we were in grade school and that made it easy for me to follow her lead in drill team. Larry was in the band which made drill team even more fun.

Larry was such a gentleman. Our dating years were delightful. He always did things like opening the door for me and without exception, would present me with an orchid corsage to wear when we attended school dances. Junior/Senior Prom dance was at Disneyland theme park. The orchid he bought me for that night was a wrist corsage with two white and pink Cymbidium Orchids to match my pink evening gown.

In the early days Prom night at Disneyland was limited to just one school at a time. Everything was so beautiful, with the girls in long, evening gowns and the boys in tuxedos or white dinner jackets.

Prom (1956)

Anyone who has attended Disneyland knows how magical the park is at night. The trees are all lit-up and music is playing. It is what every young girl dreams it will be like when she begins dating her handsome "Prince."

When Larry and I were seniors in high school he took me to a cross on a hill at Hillcrest Park. There he knelt down and proposed to me and presented me with an engagement ring. How thrilled I was to say, "Yes!"

Graduation 1956

We also got to walk together at graduation. Larry and I dated three and a half years before we married, since we were only sixteen when we started dating. We still celebrate our first-date anniversary each June eleventh. One thing Larry always did was to take me out to a lovely restaurant called Welches in Long Beach, California. There we customarily ordered Lobster Thermador. The first time he took me there I was so nervous and shy. The waiter brought a salad with a

36

whole Romaine lettuce leaf sticking out of it. I was so embarrassed because I had no idea how or what to do with it. I waited for Larry to see how I was supposed to properly eat it. He had no problem taking it down and cutting it up as part of the salad. I copied his example but I was still so nervous that I hardly ate any salad and just a bite or two of the Lobster Thermador.

By the next year and until Welches was no longer in business, I had no problem eating my salad and lobster. We were saddened when we heard it closed and we could no longer continue our customary first date anniversary at that restaurant.

After graduating from high school in 1956, I attended Fullerton Junior College in preparation for a career as a dental assistant. I received all A's in that field which is the reason the college honored me along with other women with a, "Women of Distinction" award. I worked as a dental assistant until Larry and I married.

Larry and I planned to be married on June 11, 1957 but it was too close to the end of the school year. We changed the date to August 26th of that year. We thought it would also be better because Larry would no longer be a teenager. His twentieth birthday was the day before on, August 25th. I was sad that Daddy was not here to give me away. I know he would have loved Larry and cherished the day of our wedding.

I believe God sent Kelsey Williams into my life as a substitute Father. Kelsey and his wife Bertha had no children. I think that is why Kelsey provided recreation for the teens at church. He would take us to the beach, miniature golfing and every Sunday night after church we would go to get a hamburger or sometimes, we went for his favorite delight, hot apple pie. All the kids loved him, but especially me. He and his wife Bertha were always there for me. I could always count on them to help for whatever I needed. However, Bertha did not attend the same church that we did so most of the time she was not available to go with us to any church functions or outings.

I asked Kelsey to take the place of my father and walk me down the aisle on our wedding day. He said he would be honored.

Kelsey Williams Walking me down the isle

Larry worked for the Southern California Edison Co. and I worked summer and weekends at The Chicken Dinner restaurant at Knott's Berry Farm. Knowing my mom's limited income, we were happy to pay for our wedding ourselves. However, Kelsey and Bertha owned a nursery and they provided all the flowers as a gift.

We were married in a little country church in Long Beach, California. Diane was my matron of honor and George, now her husband, was Larry's best man. My four lovely bridesmaids Lois, Anna, Patti, and Marge, wore fall colors, pastels of orange, yellow, aqua, and green. The matron of honor, Diane, was pregnant so she wore a lime-green smock of the same material that matched the bridesmaids' dresses. They all wore picture hats the same colors as their dresses and their high heels were dyed to match. The little flower girl wore pink. The little ring bearer, James, was the ministers four-year-old son.

Larry and I were trying to decide the kind of music to have at our wedding and the church recommended a professional woman harpist named, Harriet Wood. She traveled and played for weddings all over the US and later entertained regularly on the Queen Mary. When we heard how beautifully she played, we had no doubt as to the kind of music to have. She played a couple of our favorites, "Love Me Tender," and "Always."

Of course, she ended with, "Here Comes the Bride."

Our Wedding (Jay Durbin Minister)

Best of all, I had found my "Prince." And on that day, I felt like a beautiful, "Princess-Bride."

Chapter 5

Happy "Daze"

(1957-1970)

Before we married, I also worked at a dental office for a few months. It was my desire and Larry's that I stay home to be a homemaker and eventually a mother.

Larry had signed up in the service for the Navy *"TAR"* program. (Training and Administration of Reserves) Agreeing to the program, meant he could stay in one place if he took an extra year. So, four months after our lovely wedding, we were sent to Seattle, Washington for three years.

We moved into what was called Shearwater Housing for the base families (built initially as navel barracks). We had furniture provided by the military but it had absolutely no style or personality I called it, "stick" furniture. There was also a plain wood table in the kitchen.

Our Shearwater apt.
(Originally, Barracks)

The Oil heater in the
middle of the living
room. The radio is on the end
table, the coffee table same style.
also had another end table to match

There was a huge oil heater with a stovepipe extending into the ceiling in the center of the living room. I had never seen anything like that, so my first question was, "What is that?" We had to be careful not to let the oil run into the heater when we weren't using it and one time, we accidentally did just that! When we lit it, the stove got so hot it started to turn red. We called the fire department and they made everyone in the apartments stay out until it burned out all the oil. We were thankful we didn't burn down the whole place.

The curtains I made or you see the under sink had no doors so I made a curtain for it too.

More of the curtains I made + the kitchen table. The wood table looked nice when I covered it with a tablecloth.

We eventually loved living in Seattle. Everything was so green. The beauty of the trees like the Dogwood and pink and white fruit trees that bloomed in the spring and the flowers took my breath away. I especially enjoyed the purple, yellow and many other colors of the Iris and the gigantic, (around twelve inches in diameter) Chrysanthemums.

All the flowers seemed larger in size than any I had seen of the same varieties in California.

Our first piece of furniture that we bought was a desk-sewing machine. I needed it because there were no doors on the closets or cabinets. I sewed up a storm making curtains for all the closets and the kitchen window. I was so proud of everything because it did make the apartment very homey and we were very happy just having each other and a place of our own. I really enjoyed being a new bride. I even liked cooking and cleaning.

While we were in Seattle, we discussed our plans for a family. We decided it would be a good idea to wait until the last year in the service to have a baby so the Navy could pay for it but we wanted a couple years for ourselves. We got our couple years and more.

Larry finished his military service and we moved back to California. The Edison Company counted his years in the Navy as Edison's so he was able to return to work as though he had never left.

We acquired many new friends in the housing and at the church in Seattle. We were surprised and happy to hear that three of our closest friends were transferred to Southern California soon after we moved. One family was from church and became a minister in Dinuba, California. The other two families were from the housing project.

One moved to San Diego and the other to Oceanside. It was so nice to be able to visit with them here in California. We rented a nice new, apartment in Garden Grove, California. It had a swimming pool with very beautiful surroundings of plants and greenery. It was quite a leap from our Shearwater housing.

While we were still in our Garden Grove apartment, Larry and I worked for a year at the Ontario Children's home as house-parents.

We enjoyed this adventure. We were in charge of all the boys, from five years old to eighteen. Originally an older lady had the middle-aged boys but she got to where she was not physically able to continue working. So, we ended up with all the boys.

Since we were young, only twenty-five, we were able to do many fun things with them. We took them camping and to the movies and as a reward for good behavior they got to go home with us on our day off. Sometimes we would take them to Disneyland as it was so close to our apartment. We always planned something fun on that day.

I used a "merit system" rather than a "demerit." They would earn merits for the helpful things they would do and general good behavior. This system worked beautifully.

It soon became quite a contest as to who would get to go home with us.

We still had not conceived a child. After seven and a half years we were thinking that adopting a baby might be our only option. Larry was a little concerned about this process because he thought he might not be able to love a child not born to us.

After working at the Home, He said, "If I can love these boys ages five to eighteen, I can certainly love a new born baby." When our year was up and we were no longer working at the children's home we decided we would adopt. The Adoption Institute where we applied made it very easy for us to adopt. We of course, had to be financially able to care for a child and have a good home. They said, "It will likely be around nine months before a baby would be available. However, we do try to match up ethnic backgrounds." Our backgrounds evidently came up very soon. A couple weeks after we applied, I received a phone call on a Friday and they said that we could pick a little boy baby up on Monday. I said surprised, that we were contacted so soon, "Isn't this a little sudden?"

They said, "Didn't you receive your conformation letter?"

I said, "Yes, just this morning!"

They said, "Oh, we are sorry that should have been sent to you last week."

What a scurrying around that was for us as we had absolutely nothing for a baby. Larry's Dad went shopping with us. He helped us buy a crib and chest of drawers. We bought clothes, diapers, lotions and all I could think of that I would need for this little one.

Todd was four weeks and five days old when we got him from the agency. He was so adorable and so tiny, only 6 lbs. 13 oz with long brown hair. From the time he left the hospital he was in foster care. His foster mother told us Todd had just gotten over jaundice that day.

Todd Age Two Months

About a week after we brought him home, he started throwing up every time he ate. The pediatrician told us digestion is usually normal for awhile but that Todd had a projectile stomach. He said that there is a little flap that sometimes doesn't develop until a few weeks or months after a baby is born. Surgery is sometimes necessary to tack it down. We were told some children would spew vomit up to six feet. We were grateful

Todd only threw up only about a foot.

In order to avoid surgery, the doctor had me wrap Todd up tightly in a receiving blanket like a little papoose. Then he said to hold him very still for at least twenty to thirty minutes. Then I was to lay him down on his right side with a pillow propped behind his back. Many times, when he woke up, the crib would be soaked with vomit all around him. Sometimes it even ran down on to the springs of the crib. It was a total wash-down many mornings and sometimes after naps.

It was necessary to change Todd's clothes six to eight times a day. I loved dressing him though, he was so cute and really a very good baby. He managed to maintain enough weight and nutrition that surgery was not necessary. The vomiting continued, slowly getting better until it stopped at eighteen months.

During this time, we were saddened by the news that my mom's breast cancer had returned. We brought her to our home and she got to enjoy Todd. I have such sweet memories. One I cherish is, after dressing him in a little red outfit, I would watch Mama playing with Todd and hear her calling him her, "Little Red Bird."

Caring for my mom and Todd became a constant challenge. The doctors had placed tubes in both of mom's sides to keep fluid from collecting in her lungs. The need to change the bandages daily from the draining was sobering. I also continued to average a trip to the doctor's office every other week for Todd, making this a truly harrowing time of my life. The hair on the front of my head turned gray almost over night. Once as I propped my arm on the highchair to feed Todd, I fell asleep. My head dropped while I was holding the spoon. I woke up with Todd looking at me very curiously.

Sadly, we lost my Mom to breast cancer when Todd was fifteen months old. I was just twenty-eight, and I felt somewhat like and orphan having lost both parents so young.

My sister and I adored our mother. She was the epitome of integrity. I never knew Mama to say anything bad about anyone or to say a cuss word or even a, what she referred to as a, "bi-word." If I would say the word, "darn" she would say, "you might as well say the real word. All words that people use in place of cuss words are still not pleasing to the Lord," There was always scripture to back what she said so, Matthew 5: 36 & 37, says, *"And do not swear by your head, for you cannot make even one hair white or black. Simply let your yes, be "Yes" and your No, No;' Anything beyond this comes from the evil one."* (NIV) Then Mama lived the perfect example for us to follow.

I continued taking Todd to the doctor about every other week for the first two years of his life. However, on his second-year check-up, he was given a clean bill of health. The doctor said to me, "Well, I wasn't sure this kid would make it and I really didn't know if *you* would." We both laughed and gave a sigh of relief.

However, Todd's chronic problems of coordination and slow physical development continued becoming more and more obvious. He took his first steps at eighteen months. When he did begin walking and running, he could not stop himself and consequently, he bounced off walls or anything in his path. Many times, he wore a big goose egg on his head.

When friends came over to visit us and Todd would come barreling through the house and bounce off something and they would jump and gasp! "Is he, all right?"

It became so common place that we no longer noticed. I'd just say, "Oh its okay, he does that all the time."

One morning I was sitting on the floor of Todd's room, next to his chest of drawers. I asked Todd, now four years old, to hand me his pajamas so I could put them away. They were lying at his feet. He did not respond. I asked him again. Still no response. I asked him the third time, my voice now a little louder. I looked up and saw Todd's face, he said, "I---am-m-m." I saw a very confused and fearful little boy. I knew at that moment his problems were truly serious. Our pediatrician eventually diagnosed our son with an intermittent, short circuit from brain to body, similar to a seizure.

The doctor had us schedule Todd for physical therapy two or three days a week. He was to move his body back and forth in tandem with a metronome while lying on the floor. He soon began to deal better with his disability. Eventually, Todd was able to ride his tricycle and when older, a bicycle.

The pediatrician wanted Todd to start kindergarten when he was only four years of age. His birthday, October 9th made him barely old enough to start school. I was very concerned that someone could accidentally push him down and that he would be injured.

I expressed my concern to the doctor and he said, "Todd is so intelligent he is really ready to go to school." However, he said he would have Todd tested by a psychologist friend who tested children in her home so they were not aware that was the reason for their visit. She would test him for both physical and mental abilities.

After the psychologist finished testing Todd, she came in shaking her head. "No wonder he is having so many problems. Todd's intelligence range is as high as a ten year old. An example of the type of questions I asked him was, 'How are paper and coal alike?' Todd answered, 'Well, they both burn.' (I was thinking, how *are* they alike?) She continued; However, his physical co-ordination is equal to a one-and-a-half-year-old, and his actual age is four."

It was everyone's consensus that Todd would wait until the next year to attend school.

Guess what! Finally, after ten years of marriage and around Todd's third birthday, my husband and I discovered we were going to *have* a baby. The following March 16th, God blessed us with a baby girl. We named her Jill Elaine (Elaine after my sister). What a surprise gift! No girl had been born to the Lacey men as far back as anyone could remember.

I was very excited to finally be carrying a child. However, one day I picked Todd up off a chair and I felt a tare in my abdomen. It was in about my sixth month. I started to have some bleeding and I remembered my boss at work telling me about her having Placenta-Previa. She gave birth to a little girl that looked perfect but was still born. She told me babies drown in the amniotic fluid in that situation. I recognized the symptoms and called my doctor. I was panicking and the nurse said, "It's Ok Mrs. Lacey if that is the case, we will take the baby by C-section."

I told her about what my boss had experienced and she said they no longer let babies be born normally they take them by C-section and they are fine. She said however, I should be sure to let them know if I start bleeding profusely.

Right about full-term I woke in the night in a pool of blood and shaking like a leaf. Larry called the hospital and they said come immediately and for Larry to drive me himself and not to wait for an ambulance. We were told to bring the sheets so they could see the amount of blood.

I understand that surgery was rather complicated. Several doctors came in my hospital room the next day to tell me what a good job the doctor did on me. I don't know what all the complications were but I was just grateful to have my little girl.

Jill age Three Months

When we brought her home, we let Todd hold her and he seemed in awe of his tiny baby sister. I was so thrilled to have a girl. I wanted one so badly but thinking it was not possible because of the Lacey's family history of no male babies born we knew of.

One day Todd was watching me nurse Jill.

He said, "What's she doing?"

I said, "She is having her dinner."

Then Todd said, raising his little shirt up, "She can have some dinner from my shoulder." Of course, I explained God provided mommies with breasts so they can have milk (dinner) for the babies. But I thought it was so cute and sweet of him to offer.

It was good for Todd to be at home another year so he and his sister could get to know each other.

Todd had gotten a swing set for his fourth birthday. Jill was getting to be a big girl and was very quick to learn how to do things. By her second year she wanted to slide all by herself. After I helped her a couple times, she was thrilled that she could climb up the ladder and slide without help. Now Todd and Jill could play on the swing set together. They were a joy to watch.

Though Jill was only two she was already becoming bossy. Todd was playing with one of his toys and Jill grabbed it and looked at him and squealed, trying to get him to let go and he did. I had to go over and tell her, "No, that is Todd's toy." Todd was not sure how to handle her since she was a baby. I told him to tell her firmly but nicely to play with her own toys and then go find one of hers for her to play with.

Todd was five and Jill, two when God surprised us with another baby. This time on April 22nd we had a boy.

Trent age Two Months

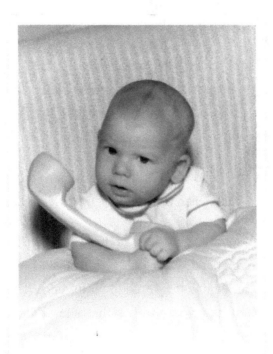

Thank God this pregnancy was uneventful except I had to have another C-section as my doctor would not let her patients have a normal birth when they had gone through a C-section before. I guess it was a good thing too as she said my uterus was too thin to carry anymore children. If I did carry another baby it could kill me and the baby. So, I was glad she insisted I have the surgery again.

Trent was energetic and comical and a tease from the time he could walk and talk. Trent kept me laughing almost continually.

One time I told him to get ready to go to town. He was not yet three and already able to dress himself. He came out on the patio where I was and said, "I ready to go mama" I looked up and he had put his pants on his head, his shirt on his bottom, wearing my boots and holding my purse. It cracked me up. I said stay right there and I went in got the camera and took his picture. I could go on about situation after situation through-out his life where he pulled things like that and he still does.

Maybe we should have named him, "Isaac" which means laughter. Our family was now complete.

Joyce (Grammer) Lacey

Chapter 6

Kids, Kids and More Kids

(1970-1988)

Until I became pregnant with Trent, I worked in the Hunt Foods laboratory during the tomato season. My job was to record any impurities and mold in the products by looking through a microscope. I enjoyed working in the lab and worked there for eight seasons. I was offered a managing position but I said, "No" realizing it would be too much while raising three children.

The seasons kept getting longer and longer. They started with just two months and then it went to three and by the time I had Jill, they had extended work to four months. I heard it was to be six months the next season. I was working graveyard so I could care for Todd and Jill in the day time. I would go home on my night lunch hour, to nurse Jill. I only lived about a mile away. Then I got pregnant again. I realized it would be more than I could handle if I continued to work at Hunts so I quit.

To help with the finances I began making things to sell. I made stuffed dogs, "Around the World Dolls", "Raggedy Ann and Andy" and "Holly Hobby" dolls. I took orders at my beauty shop and when my friends saw my work, they would order from me too.

For my niece and my daughter, I made a set of, "Around the World Dolls." These Dolls depicted children from Holland, Africa, Asia, Switzerland, and Spain and an Indian or Native American as we say now.

I made a set of stuffed dogs for another niece.

Trent loved the stuffed bulldog I made for him so much he would carry it around by its ear, and he would sit on it while watching television.

Todd and Trent got a "Raggedy Andy" and Jill, a "Raggedy Ann" and a "Holly

Hobby" doll. I was really getting into sewing as the children were growing up so I made many of their clothes and several Christmas gifts.

In March of 1975, Larry was transferred to the San Bernardino Edison office and we moved to Yucaipa, California. Todd was ten, Jill just turned seven and Trent was almost five. Though I said I never wanted to live on a hill we really enjoy our new home in the North Bench area. Our home is on 1 .57 acres on which the kids could run and play.

We moved to Yucaipa, and we always look for a church home. I was raised my whole life in the Church of Christ so we settled with that denomination in Yucaipa. I began teaching bible class at church on Wednesday nights for the junior high girls. These girls were so willing to learn and share their particular needs and teen problems. We had great times getting together and providing the elderly from church with a basket of flowers on May Day. On Christmas, we would go caroling at the Mobile Home parks. We also performed music programs for parents and friends. For fun we took the girls on outings to the beach. I cherish the time I spent with these girls.

From Kindergarten through fifth grade I was a room mother for my kid's classes in the public school, and for four years I, JoAnn Kraut, and Lin Richter were in charge of what we called, "The Christmas Craft Store." We and other mothers would make items to sell and then we would open the store for the kids to buy Christmas gifts especially for their parents. Sometimes we got a gift back from our child that we had made but we didn't mind because the kids were so delighted to be able to buy gifts for their parents.

Lin was also my neighbor and good friend. She nominated me for the Founders Day Award because of my work with children.

The night of the Founders Day program I was backstage helping to organize those participating in the program. I was dressed in a T-shirt and pedal pushers because I had no idea I was going to be honored or seen. I was very surprised and humbled and I also felt a little embarrassed to be inappropriately dressed when I received the award.

The next year Jill started the sixth grade and we entered her in Panorama Christian School in Yucaipa. Two years later Trent started attending there too. Todd was starting high school and Panorama did not have a high school at that time. It did expand yearly to include High School so Jill and Trent both graduated from there. My husband

Larry was President of the school while our children were in attendance there.

The kids had joined the Flying Fish swim team in Yucaipa, Jill especially enjoyed swimming. She developed her time well enough to qualify for the Jr. Olympics to be held in Florida. Jill has scoliosis but never before had been a problem while swimming. One time however, she was practicing the fly and she pulled muscles in her back. Sadly, she was not able to continue preparing for the Olympics. We were all disappointed. We had great plans for my sister and her family who lived in Baton Rouge, Louisiana, to attend the event with us. Elaine's in-laws lived in Tampa, Florida and we also planned to visit them while in their area.

During the time the kids were on the swim team I became a team transport mom.

Every night for many years I hauled a station wagon full of kids to swim practice in San Bernardino, JoAnn, another mother and dear friend, helped take some kids too.

Todd was fourteen when he started on the swim team. It was hard for him to play catch-up and he said he was tired of almost always coming in last so he only swam one year. Jill and Trent remained on the team until the age limit of eighteen.

The teen years were a very difficult time for our family. Todd had many emotional melt-downs. He was so unhappy with his life, not being able to do the things he wanted to do. I found that God's word never rang truer than when I looked back at those times of crisis. His promise that, *"...God causes all things to work together for good to those who love God and those who are called according to His purpose."* (Romans 8:28) (NASB) God used this time of difficulty to grow each of us spiritually. Larry and I became more aware of the person of the Holy Spirit and His power. We observed the compassion of Jill and Trent toward people that have special needs and with people in general. Todd is more at peace even though he has never been able to have the life he would have preferred, but a life with many who love him and, *"Love never fails."* I Corinthians 13:8 (NIV)

***

During the time the kids were in high school and then college, Larry and I managed an Antique/Thrift store for Panorama School. We enjoyed the three-and-a-half years we worked at the store though it was pretty much a twenty-four-seven job.

We opened the shop the day after Larry retired. He became the bookkeeper and I took care of the customer's, antiques and the incoming donated items. Half of the store was thrift items and the other half was divided off for vendors who had antiques and others who sold new and hand-crafted items.

Many interesting people came to shop. Some loved the antiques and others enjoyed the new and crafted items. Some just liked to look around in the store. There were some shoplifters too. I finally realized a lady who regularly came in always carried a bag that was flat but left with it bulging.

I would like to have told her that she could come to me if she really needed something and I would let her have it. I wanted to explain that the store was to help the school and the kids that could not afford tuition. However, she noticed I saw her bag and she left quickly and never came back again.

I could never stand the scent of most thrift stores, so I was determined Panorama Mall would not have a musty smell. I took all the clothes in the thrift area home to wash or I sent them to the dry cleaners. I wanted everything we sold to look like new.

I also sold packages of potpourri so the store would have a pleasant aroma.

Joyce (Grammer) Lacey

Chapter 7

Our Nest Now Empty

(1998-2004)

It seemed strange to have the children "fly the coop." We had to face the fact though. The first to leave the nest was our daughter Jill. She attended Pepperdine University. While there Jill was invited to Dean Mitchell's home for a weekly Bible study. Mick Mitchell was now living in Malibu. He also attended his parents Bible study.

Afterwards, Mick and Jill would go to a coffee shop to talk. They had known each other for some time because he had been the principle at Panorama Christian School in Yucaipa and attended the same church while we were there.

Mick, was helping his father, Carl Mitchell, (Dean of Students at Pepperdine University), prepare villas in Italy. Students could attend one year of school in another country. To qualify they needed to be on the "Deans List" by achieving a high-grade point average.

Mick's dad and mom took a group of students to Italy during Jill's sophomore year. She was so excited to be one of the thirty-eight who qualified.

Before going to Italy, Mick came to us and asked our permission to ask Jill out on a date. He asked us because of their age difference. If we had any objections, he said he would not pursue dating her any further. We were happy to tell him; though fifteen years was a big age difference, it was perfectly alright with us as long as our daughter was in agreement.

Jill and Mick discovered that they *were* very fond of each other while in beautiful, romantic Italy. Their love grew and when they returned home, Mick, asked for Jill's hand in marriage.

Larry and I were delighted that they wanted to marry. We love Mick and we were happy to say, "Yes." Jill went back to school and two years later Mick and Jill were married at the Yucaipa Christian Church. Mick's dad, also a minister, officiated.

We were pleased we kept the phone number of Harriet Wood, the professional harpist who played for our wedding thirty-one years before and that she still lived in the same place. She told us she performed during lunch on the Queen Mary. We went with Jill and Mick to listen to her. They were very impressed with her performance and ask if she would play for their wedding and she agreed. What a blessing and a surprise to find her and know she would be able to play for Mick and Jill's wedding too. Jill asked my sister Elaine to sing for the wedding. I usually sang with a quartet known as, "One in Spirit." Elaine took my place in the quartet. I recorded the Lord's prayer with Ms. Wood accompanying me on the harp and we taped it for the wedding.

Jill's bridesmaids were dressed in pastels and lace like beautiful southern belles and carrying white lace parasols. Jill's dress was white satin with lace sleeves and long train. The back was open and four strings of pearls were attached to a satin flower at the middle of the back. On either side of the flower, the four strands of pearls draped across her back. She wore a big white picture hat in keeping with the southern belle theme.

After the wedding, Mick surprised her with a horse and carriage. When it arrived to pick them up at the church, Jill cried tears of joy.

As they rode down Yucaipa Boulevard, they looking every bit the "Prince" and "Princess" as they waved to everyone on their way to the reception at the Church of Christ in town.

Trent, our youngest son, was next to leave the nest. He also attended Pepperdine for one and half years but decided he really wasn't ready to continue school at that time.

He decided instead to drop out and go to Europe with some friends. He had quite a time surviving there. He had to do whatever necessary to live. I believe it was good for him. It helped him to mature and when he came home, he was ready to return to college.

Trent finished his AA degree at our Crafton Hills College in town. While there he enjoyed acting and was in several plays including, "Fiddler on the Roof." He played the boyfriend to one of Tevye's daughters. Next, he attended Orange Coast College and then transferred to San Bernardino State University where he received his Bachelor of Arts degree.

Trent was working at a restaurant and this beautiful girl came in regularly and would talk to him. Trent asked her out and they began dating. Her name was Jackie Eden.

To get acquainted, Trent and Jackie, Larry and I attended concerts together and sometimes we went out to dinner. We soon realized what our son saw in this lovely girl.

Trent told us he had asked Jackie to marry him. He proposed to her on one of the lifeguard shacks at Newport beach. They both loved the beach and decided to be married there.

The wedding had a Hawaiian theme. It was a gorgeous day. The bridesmaids were in solid blue, tropically-designed, dresses. The men wore Hawaiian shirts and leis. Jackie looked every bit the "Hawaiian Princess" in her crown of orchids as she walked down the sand aisle to Trent, her "Island Prince." My husband and I were very happy to welcome this beautiful bride into our family.

Jackie is a teacher and has received her Master's degree. She recently has been teaching science for all grades at her school.

Keeping up with wife Jackie, Trent received his master's degree a few years ago. He taught Jr. High students, math and science. Recently he worked at a school with children who have discipline problems. He has just been promoted to assistant principal for the coming year at a new school.

Lastly, our adopted son Todd moved out. It was hard for him. He was never able hold down a job because of the "short circuit" in his brain. When he would get a job, the boss would think he was just goofing off when he just stood still and did nothing. He would rather they thought that than that he had a disability.

He now lives in a board and care facility. He started attending Team House, a government resource for people needing a place to go for counseling and to learn life skills. There he met a girl named Cindy. She has been his girlfriend for about fourteen years. She also lives in a board and care facility in another town. They want to get married but her parents said that she is ill so often it would be unfair to them both to try to care for each other. We agree with them. We love Cindy she is truly like another daughter-in-law to us. In fact, she said one day, "Is it OK with you both if I call you Mom and Dad?" We said that would be perfectly fine with us.

In 2000, my husband and I felt led to attend the Christian Church in Yucaipa. We were able to put our talents to better use there. The people at Yucaipa Christian Church are very loving and we enjoy the wonderful fellowship. I sing in the choir and also on

Tuesday ladies' class I sing with the girls that lead worship. I am so grateful to be able to use my talent for the Lord.

We often take Todd and Cindy to church with us. About once a month, Cindy's parents take Todd and Cindy out to dinner and sometimes to their home in Victorville.

For many years during the summer, we rented a beach house at Newport for our family to enjoy. Several times we had invited Lance and Ailene and their family to come and visit us while we were there. They were never able to come until this one particular year. Through them God provided a gift of love for us in a way we could not have imagined.

My sister Elaine who lived in Baton Rouge, Louisiana, had been fighting breast cancer for some time. She passed away that summer on August, 28, 2004. We just got back from visiting her a couple weeks before our vacation at the beach. We knew her cancer was diagnosed at stage four, but we hoped to have had more time before going back to Louisiana. It so happened that Lance and Ailene, friends of ours from church, were with us when we got the news of my sister's passing. They told us they had free air miles that they were not going to be able to use so we could have them. It would have been impossible for us to go right back to Louisiana had they not blessed us with those tickets. God is good.

Harry, a long-time friend said he would stay at the beach house until we returned. God continually shows how faithful He is to His promise that says, *"Never will I will never leave you; never will I forsake you."* (NIV)

Chapter 8

Friendship; God's Special Gifts

"Just as Lotion and Fragrance give sensual delight, a sweet friendship

refreshes the soul,"

Proverbs 27: 9, (The Msg. Bible)

I find that this quote from the Bible expresses my deep emotional feelings on friendship. When I pause and think about the incredible friends I have had, I realize they were, and continue to be, valuable treasures that God provided to comfort and enrich my life.

From the time I moved to Fullerton. At age five until my father died when I was eleven, Lucille Massey was a neighbor who lived in a very big house across the street and next to Amerage Park. Her grandmother lived with them and took care of her, because her mom and dad both worked.

Her family owned work horses and they hired man named Joe, to keep their field plowed. When we were about seven, Joe would let Lucille and me ride on the horses while he plowed the field. The horse's backs weren't very comfortable but we thought riding on them was great fun.

One-time Joe brought a Palomino horse to her house and penned it up in her back yard. I thought, *"This is the most beautiful horse I have ever seen."* I just had to get on him. We were not supposed to go into the pen but I asked Lucille to bring a box over by the horse so I could climb on his back. I got on him bareback, no bridles or anything. I am grateful to God that the horse was gentle and didn't mind me trying to ride him around the pen. I told Lucille I would never do that again. We might get in trouble.

Lucille had a big black walnut tree and we would try and try to crack those walnuts. I think we managed to crack a few with a big hammer, but we decided it wasn't worth the effort. I remember looking up in that walnut tree one time and I saw a huge, yellow and black-striped, Writing Spider in its web. I actually thought it was beautiful. We were afraid of it and I guess that was a good thing as I understand they are poisonous.

When Lucille and I were around eight and nine we always seemed to be selling something. She had a plum tree and we would pick the plums to sell. Her father would help us climb up on the roof to pick some of them because the tree hung over the roof of the house.

She also had chickens. At that same time, we got the bright idea to gather up chicken feathers, wash and comb them and sell them as fashion accessories for dolls. I said Lucille, "Let's go get your storybook dolls, they have feathers in their hats. We can use them to show one-way people can use them."

She said, "OK that sounds like a good idea."

Well, the chicken feathers weren't a big seller but we did sell lots of plums.

72

Though it would gross me out today, as kids we thought it was very funny to see Lucille's grandmother wring a chicken's neck and watch it run around with its head off. Her grandmother would pick the feathers off, and then take the chicken in the house to fry it immediately. I can still taste the freshly-cooked chicken. I have never since eaten any that tastes as scrumptious as chicken prepared fresh off the farm.

The memories I have playing at Lucille's are of freedom at play and genuine fun times. We still stay in touch with each other.

During these same years, Jean Scranton was our neighbor. She and my sister Elaine were best friends. I was four when we moved behind her house. Many times, I would go to her house with my sister. But I would play in her back yard sometimes by myself.

I loved playing at her house. She had a huge swing that her father strung up over a very high tree branch. The rope was so long we could swing ever so high. She also had a cat, named Jasper. Well, actually he belonged to the whole neighborhood but I think he liked the Scratton's best because they really loved him and he usually stayed there.

I also had a friend Kay, who I met in kindergarten. Her dad built her a playhouse. We played for hours pretending we were the mommy and daddy and our dolls were our babies.

Kay took dancing lessons and she taught me how to do the hula, and a few other dances. When we were in the fourth grade and after we had been practicing the hula at her house, she said, "Joyce for our school talent show you should sing, *Little Brown Gal.* I will dance the hula to it. OK?"

I said, "Yes that will be fun." So, we did and quite well, as I remember.

Her family owned a black-and-white TV. I was ten. Hardly anyone had a television in 1949. We would watch the Beanie and Cecil puppet show. It was exciting to be entertained in a new way.

One time when I was spending the night at Kay's her mom cooked an artichoke. I had never even seen one. It was quite a new experience for me. I thought it was so fun to dip the leaves in butter bite down on a leaf and slide it through my teeth to be able to eat the pulp inside of each leaf. I even liked the taste. I was not so sure that I would, considering it was such a strange-looking vegetable.

When we were in the fifth grade, Kay called me and said, "Would you like to go to Catalina with me and my family."

I said, "Yes, I think that would a lot of fun. Thank you."

On the Santa Catalina boat ride over to the island we saw flying fish. I couldn't believe my eyes. I was actually seeing fish fly.

When we got to the island, we rode the glass bottom boat. It was amazing to be able to see fish swim underneath it. After our boat ride, Kay and I went shopping and bought butterfly-wing rings and necklaces. They would be rare now because it is not legal to make jewelry out of butterfly wings anymore.

Several times over the years Kay invited me to go to the mountains to play in the snow. We had such fun tobogganing down the hills. Someone in her family owned a cabin at Forest Home. Living in Fullerton made snow quite a treat.

I missed Kay when I moved to Buena Park. We had been friends from kindergarten thru fifth grade. Friendship with Kay gave me opportunities to do things that I would not have been able to experience in my usual circle of family and friends.

When I was thirteen, my sister Elaine, married Joe Liuzzo and moved to Michigan. She was not just my sister but also my best friend. In 1964, Jean, (Elaine's friend) and I became much closer. I missed my sister and Jean helped fill the void, she became like a sister to me. After I married and had children, Jean and I could also share things going on in their lives. In 1975 we moved to Yucaipa and she often comes and stays a few days with us. We play dominoes, cards, go out to dinner and/or a movie. We have a great time together. I am so thankful for friends like Jean, who I can enjoy, pray with, and cry with. I also know I can talk to her about things of a personal nature, knowing it will be kept in strict confidence. I have known Jean more years than anyone else. I was about four when we moved behind her in Fullerton. She has gone to be with the Lord.

I have another "Jean" friend her name is Jean Stafford and we have been friends since junior high. Jean is a year younger, so we were together more during high school and at church functions and outings. Jean is my dependable friend. She is always in attendance and willing to help with any family get together or celebration. She too is like a sister to me. We try to celebrate our birthdays together every year at Knott's Berry Farm's Chicken Dinner Restaurant where we worked as teenagers. At Knotts we worked in teams of two, but Jean and I were not teamed up together.

However, God provided another friend for me to team up with. Her name is Patti. We had great fun working together at Knotts. We liked working in the south wing of the restaurant where mostly businessmen were seated. There were lots of tables for two or four and those men were the best tippers. One day we got so excited when we counted our tips. We had each made twenty dollars. In the fifties that was a lot of money.

Patti and I loved going to fancy restaurants with our boyfriends. It was customary back then for the boys to pay for everything when on a date. I loved Patti's wit. She kept me laughing and still does whenever and wherever we go. Patti and Jean were next door neighbors growing up. The three of us still try to get together once a year. Sometimes we meet at Patti's lovely home. We would go to lunch to catch up on all that had happened in our lives during the past year. I am so thankful for these forever friends.

New friends have also blessed my life

My husband was discharged from the Navy in 1960 and we moved from Seattle to Garden Grove, California and then to Fullerton, California. Our new friends have continually uplifted, comforted and expressed their love to both my husband and me.

I believe it is important to emphasize the impact good friends bring into ones' life, especially during times of need. One of those times in my life occurred after we moved to Fullerton.

Reta Hutchins and her husband, Tom, were wonderful neighbors. Todd had so much fun playing with their two boys, Scott and Tim.

One day I noticed Todd had a rash that looked like measles. I was pregnant with Trent and I knew it was important to get Todd to the doctor – not only for him – but I realized there was a danger if I got measles while I was pregnant.

I had just laid Jill down for her nap. I called Reta to see if she could baby sit so I wouldn't have to wake her. Reta wasn't home. I kept checking her driveway to see if she had returned home, but no. Just as I was reaching down into the crib to pick up Jill and take her with me, Reta popped in the door and said, "Joyce do you need me to baby-sit?"

I said, "How did you know?" I had been saying something like, *Lord please have Reta get home before I have to leave.* Reta said, "Well, I was shopping at the mall in La Habra, and I just kept hearing, *'Go home, Joyce needs you!"* That was the first time I had experienced the working of the Holy Spirit in such a dramatic way. Though I did not understand at that time much about the Holy Spirit or how He operated, I knew God had in some way relayed the message to Reta.

When we moved to Yucaipa in 1975, I experienced the true meaning of the *gift of hospitality*. Harry and Alene Whitt invited my husband and me to their lovely home for homemade pie and coffee to get acquainted and welcome us to the church family. I learned later that Alene always had pies prepared and froze them to have on hand to serve new people that came to church. Consequently, many felt encouraged to place membership as Larry and I did.

She and Harry have a daughter, Laura who is twelve years older than her brother David. Our daughter Jill and David are the same age only seven at that time. She and David attended Panorama Christian School from the sixth grade and until they graduated from High school. Alene was the secretary at that school. Sadly, the year before David and Jill graduated, she went to be with the Lord after a long battle with cancer. She was a very good friend. I appreciated her hospitality and admired her ability to organize everything so well. Romans 12: 6a & 13 states, *"And since we have gifts that differ according to the grace given to us, let each exercise them accordingly...13, contributing to the needs of the saints, practicing hospitality."* (NASB)

Harry is still our dear friend. He is always there when we need him. He has always come to our rescue with a cheerful, willing heart.

Meeting Mary Gauer was truly a, "God thing." One morning I took my kids to the doughnut shop after swim practice. In walked this lady that said, "I heard you have pamphlets for Marriage Encounter here." "The shop owner said, "No, I'm sorry we don't."

Overhearing the conversation, I said, "Ma'am, I just happen to have some in my purse." I invited her to sit down with us. In the course of our conversation we discovered that my son Todd, and her daughter, Dawn, were both in the emotionally handicapped class at the high school. Getting to know Mary was such a blessing. She taught me about the Holy Spirit and His purpose in our lives.

Mary had many trials of her own. She has three children. Her oldest daughter Dawn, has cerebral palsy and epilepsy. Her son, John, was born with a club foot that had to be amputated and he now has an artificial leg. She was blessed with another daughter, Heather, that has no physical problems.

Mary is such an inspiration to me. Through her I learned how to hear from God. I always knew God spoke to us through His word, but I did not understand about the Holy Spirit or how to give God the glory for the good things He did through us.

For example; One day, as we were talking Mary said, "The Lord told me to take some groceries to my friend who is very sick."

I said, "Mary, how do you know *God* told you to do that? Do you hear an audible voice?"

She said, "No, it's a thought."

I said, "Then how do you *know* that it was God?"

She said, very simply, "Well, *I* would never think of that."

She explained further, "When I went to the store, I thought, *"Now what should I get her Lord?"* The first thought that came to my mind was, *"liver."*

She said, "I was so surprised that I said, *'LIVER!'* right out loud. I embarrassed myself, but I bought the liver." Mary continued, "When I got to Joan's house, Joan was so amazed and asked how I knew to buy liver. She said the doctor told her to eat liver two times a week because she was very anemic." Mary again shared the story at Joan's house and we all had a good laugh.

A good verse in scripture to explain hearing God's voice is, John 10: 2-5, (NIV)

"The man who enters by the gate is the Shepherd of the sheep. The watchman opens the gate for Him, and the sheep listen to His voice. He calls His own sheep by name and leads them out. When He has brought out all his own, He goes on ahead of them, and His sheep follow Him because they know His voice. But they will never follow a stranger; in fact, they will run away from him because they do not recognize his voice." Verse 14 Jesus says, *"I am the good Shepherd and I know my sheep and My sheep know Me."*

Mary also taught me an important principle on hearing from God. That is, not to give myself credit for things I do for others. I need to give God the glory for all good things I do. James 1:17 says, *"Every GENEROUS ACT and every perfect gift is from above, coming down from the Father."* (HCSB) [Emphasis mine]

I realize now that the Holy Spirit dwells in me to communicate God's will. I no longer say, *"I* took food over to a friend, or *I* visited a sick friend." I try to speak as Mary does, and say, "The Lord impressed on my heart that I need to visit, or take food to a friend."

Another friend I have known since our boys were in kindergarten together. Her name is Barbara Wiggins. Barbara is my encourager friend. She helped type my book about our adopted son Todd. She supported all my efforts to develop stories that will glorify my Father in heaven. I get such praise from her that I am uplifted and continue my writing when I feel discouraged and think I should just quit trying.

From the time our kids were very young we enjoyed the friendship of Jon and Barbara Whan. Their kids, Jay and Jeff, are about the same ages as Todd, Jill and Trent.

We camped with the Whans at Carpenteria Beach many times. Then we decided to rent a beach house together at Newport every summer. The house was only about a block from the ocean. Our kids became more like siblings than friends. We felt like one big family. Many fond memories were generated from both of these beach areas.

At Carpenteria we walked to town and especially enjoyed the antique shops and eating at some of the restaurants there. At both places we loved walking in the moonlight and enjoying the warm ocean breeze. At Newport, our walk usually ended up at 31 Flavors for our favorite ice cream. Sometimes we took in a movie.

Larry is a great cook and he fixed dinner many times for everyone who came to visit. Some friends came to stay for a few days. Sometimes Larry and Jon would decide to cook something together. We happened to have these huge cans of blackberries that another friend had given us and they thought it would be really good to make an enormous berry cobbler. So, they did. Well to put it mildly it was not even edible! But we all had a great time teasing them about their inability to bake.

Barbara and Jon's kids and our kids loved to make fun of me in my big beach hat and my navy and white polka dot, one-piece bathing suit. They also loved to get me in a situation where I was vulnerable, like the time they talked me into going out in the ocean, on a raft. They were all good swimmers. They swam next to the raft and taking hold of the side-ropes made the ocean much rougher than it actually was. That was a ride I will never forget. I threatened them within an inch of their lives if they didn't take me back to shore. They laughed so hard but *I* was not laughing. However, *not letting them know*, I did get a kick out of their amusement over it all.

I cannot think of more pleasant and enjoyable times than when we were with the Whans. They are so dear to my heart. Even when all our kids were grown with children of their own we still enjoyed the beach house at Newport though the Whan family were not renting with us anymore. However, they did come to visit often.

When I think of *recreation,* I think of the time spent with the Whan Family. Our spirits were definitely refreshed. When I think of them, Proverbs 18:24b says, *"...there is a friend who sticks closer than a brother."* (NIV)

Larry and I walked every morning. Sometimes we waded in the water along the ocean's edge. Other times we walked the sidewalks to town. Many mornings we would stop at Malarkey's our favorite place for breakfast, or a coffee shop, or one of the several restaurants by the bay.

***

Archieva (Archie) Huff, what a dear friend, she came a few times to visit us at the beach. I considered her my spiritual mother. When I had a biblical question, I could count on her to direct me to the appropriate scripture for the answer. The times I felt spiritually depleted she would counsel, uplift and encourage me with her words of wisdom. This passage from, Proverbs 27:9, comes to mind when I think of her: *"The heartfelt counsel of a friend is as sweet as perfume and incense."* (NLT)

She also filled in as natural mother to me and like a grandmother to our children. She took care of Todd several times and gave him odd jobs around her house.

She sent money anonymously for Jill's wedding. We eventually realized it came from Archie because of the many comical cards the money would come in. It so obviously depicted her personality. With her donation of love, we were able to buy Jill's wedding dress and also the dress I wore.

When Jill and Trent were ready to apply for college, she wrote letters of recommendation to Pepperdine University on their behalf. When Jill went to Italy, Archie gave her money to ride the Euro-Rail.

She was willing to help with the kids whenever and in whatever way needed. She has since gone to be with the Lord and we all miss her love and sweet smile.

I could go on and on about so many more precious friends God placed in my life that helped me grow, emotionally and spiritually. However, I wanted to mention just a few specific examples of friends who unknowingly, assisted me in my desire to be a more loving and devoted child of God.

I believe one of God's many ways of manifesting His love for us is by providing, through the avenue of friendships, fathers, mothers, sisters, and brothers.

Before I got to the end of this memoir, I wanted to honor those who contributed so much during my life by their friendship the bible says: "Proverbs 17:17 (NIV)

"A friend loves at all times" and I certainly found that to be true.

Chapter 9

Princess-Bride Again!

(2005-2020)

The years 2005-2006 were pretty uneventful. But in 2007, our children honored us by hosting a fantastic dinner party for our fiftieth wedding anniversary. It was a four- hour tour around the bay on the Icon Yacht that holds dinner parties for weddings, anniversaries and the like at Newport Beach.

We enjoyed a hundred and twenty guests, both old friends and new. At the reception I had them play a special song that the little children could dance to with the adults. First, Peyton danced with me and he almost wore me out. In the song it says to, "clap your hands and stomp your feet." Even Vivian, our granddaughter, who was only two, could do the dance with me. I had such fun. A memory I will cherish forever.

A dear friend and famous Gospel singer Vern Jackson sang, *"Remember When"* and *"Because."* And God provided the most beautiful weather and the most gorgeous sunset I've ever seen. Pictures of our Anniversary at the end.

Larry and I renewed our vows. As I looked into the face of my wonderful "Prince

Charming" husband, it was a thrill to repeat the vows I had said to him so many years ago. Again, I felt like a "Princess-Bride again."

Our Trip Around the U.S.

We bought a new car in March of 2009 then in September of that year and we decided to travel across country. We took Harry, our long-time friend, as far as Virginia to his daughter Laura's. We enjoyed this trip immensely. On the way we went through the Creation Museum, In Texas. It was closed but a caretaker who doubled as a tour guide opened it up for us and took us on a private tour. We were amazed at all the displays that showed how the earth was before the Fall.

The guide told us God originally made the earth similar to a terrarium. The Bible records that no rain ever fell, but, *"a mist used to rise from the earth and water the whole surface of the ground."* Genesis 2:6 (NASB) Everything was perfect.

At the museum they try to duplicate the same environment as the Garden of Eden. We saw a comparison of snake venom before the Fall then after. When tested under perfected conditions, using an increase of atmospheric pressure, oxygen and carbon-dioxide ratios, the venom was no longer poisonous. We could actually see the difference.

When we got to Harry's daughter, Laura, and her family's home, we stayed a couple days with them and visited Mount Vernon and the Episcopal Church where George and Martha Washington worshiped. Since we had been to Washington D.C. before, we didn't re-visit the monuments and other tourist sites.

We left Harry at his daughter's as she was to bring him back to California. We then traveled on up the east coast to Connecticut to visit my niece PattiJo and her husband Mick and their son, Cody. We stayed there a couple days and they took us to New York and to see the Statue of Liberty. We could not go into the statue as it was fully booked. However, at Ellis Island we enjoyed learning about the history of the island. We found the Lacey family name recorded on a plaque noting people as they entered the United States.

From my niece's we traveled on up to Sandwich, Massachusetts at Cape Cod we enjoyed a bowl of clam chowder at Seafood Sam's. It was scrumptious.

On our way up the coast we were in awe of all the beautiful autumn leaves. I was amazed at the colors of all the hills; they looked like mounds of multi-colored pompoms.

When we got to Maine my first thought was, they must have Lobster Thermador on their menu here. We found the famous floating, seafood, restaurant, Di Millo's, and we went there for dinner. We asked the waitress if they served Lobster Thermador explaining that we annually celebrated our *first date* anniversary on June 11th, at a restaurant that served it but several years ago had gone out of business. We had not found any-place that served it since and we liked to reminisce while eating our favorite lobster dish.

The waitress apologized and said, "No, but we have Lobster Pie." She said it was very similar. We were so thrilled when we tasted it because it was the same sauce but it wasn't served in a lobster half shell. Neither was it a pie as it had no crust. It was just that marvelous sauce with big chunks of lobster we loved so much. It really made our day, even though it was in September and not our *first date* anniversary.

On our way home we traveled to Bentonville, Arkansas to see Ray and Cherry Bonser some dear friends that used to attend church with us in Yucaipa.

We heard Ray had a heart attack. We went to the hospital to visit him. He was doing quite well and still is so we are thankful to God for his healing.

We then traveled home and didn't stop again to see any more sights as our time was getting short.

Larry takes Todd camping at Carpenteria every year. I usually stay at home but in 2012 and 2013 my good friend Jean Brown and I decided we should take a vacation too and stay in a hotel in Simi Valley. There we visited my daughter Jill and her family and enjoyed the area. We only stayed for about three days. We had a good time playing dominoes and cards in the big conference room when it is not occupied. Going Shopping was fun and sometimes we had dinner out or did what ever we wanted to do. I love spending time with Jean.

Chapter 10

Wisdom Gained from this Journey

W hat have I learned throughout all the years? I learned I have an incredible husband, who stuck by me through all the valleys, when many men would have left.

Also, I learned to be grateful for the precious gifts God gave Larry and me:

First, He gave us our adopted son, Todd, our precious, adorable, and longed-for-child of many years. Secondly, we had, Jill, our compassionate, intelligent, talented, and beautiful daughter. Our third gift, Trent, is our handsome, smart, comical and loving son.

God has added more to our family. Our son Todd has a girlfriend, Cindy. They met at a government run facility that tries to give adults an opportunity to develop any skills they might have. Like Todd, she lives in a board-and-care home for individuals with special needs. They started dating about fourteen years ago. Cindy is a sweet, loving, polite, and sensitive girl, and we love her very much. We feel blessed to have come to know her and we think of her as another daughter. Sadly, a couple years later Cindy died with pneumonia. Todd has been very sad since. Our constant prayer is that he will find peace in the love of God.

Our daughter Jill blessed our family with her very attractive husband, Mick. He is a kind, gentle, Christian man and a wonderful father. They have given us two grandsons, Shane, now twenty-six years old, and Preston who is twenty-three.

Shane is a handsome, quick-minded, and loving young man. He graduated from Pepperdine in 2014. He married Amber on July 6th of the same year. They dated about three years.

Amber, Shane's wife, is as lovely on the inside as she is gorgeous on the outside. She is a multi-talented young lady who loves homemaking and even cuts Shane's hair and trims his beard. Her desire is to be a stay-at-home mom when they have children. She is also an artist.

Shane and Amber were married July fifth 2014, and on Christmas we learned that they were going to have a baby July, 2015, possibly on their anniversary? They now have, three boys. Jadon, age four, Caleb age three, and Noah soon to be one.

Jill and Mick's youngest son, Preston, is my good looking, smart, game-competitor, grandson. He likes to challenge me to play cards, dominos and other games. He graduated with honors from Trinity home school, high in 2013. He participated in "Mock Trials" his junior and senior years. Out of thirty-two schools in Ventura County, he was awarded first place as a bailiff. The next year, he again won first place as the court bailiff out of all the top schools in Northern California. He's finished his first year in College. He took mission training in Oregon and had the opportunity to go to the Philippines to teach and help orphans there.

Our youngest son, Trent, added three blessings also, first of all, his wife Jackie. I could have searched the world over and would never have found a more perfect daughter-in-law. Jackie is beautiful and has an outgoing and loving personality and she is a great wife and mother. We so appreciate the love and consideration she consistently shows

Larry and me. One of the thoughtful things she does for us is prepare picture albums/books and calendars of special occasions to recall our family get-togethers. Trent and Jackie added two grandchildren to our family, Peyton who is eighteen and attending Cal-Poly in Northern California, and Vivian who is fourteen and in her first year of High School.

Peyton is my cute, brown-eyed, ball of fire. He is smart as a whip and a big tease. He enjoyed playing basketball for the Emmanuel Baptist Church when young.

He likes to play the guitar and drums.

Vivian liked cheerleading at the Baptist Church, especially for her brother's team. She likes drama and loves to sing and take part in plays. She is my longed for, adorable, tender-hearted, and thoughtful granddaughter. Now in High School she is in Water Polo and their team came in second in their league. She also likes to sing in the choir at school.

Best of all, I have learned to a greater degree how great and attentive God has been throughout my journey here on earth. I cannot imagine my life without the love of the Father, Son, and the Holy Spirit who is also my Comforter, Helper and daily Guide.

Joyce (Grammer) Lacey

Chapter 11

Miracles: No Problem

"With God all things are possible." Mathew 19:26b (KJV)

I almost did not write this chapter. I was so excited to finally publish my memoir that I had not realized I didn't write anything about the last three or four years.

I find that I usually hear from God at night when I go to bed. I guess it is because it is quiet and no distractions. So that night after I already sent my manuscript in to the publishers I hear "Joyce you haven't written the latest chapter in your life" I thought That's right I am leaving out possibly the most important years of all.

In 2017 I was diagnosed with stage four tonsil cancer. Strangely, I was not alarmed. Somehow, I knew everything would be alright. However, the treatments were stressful though not painful. I had to take the radiation and Erbitux (similar to chemo) treatments five days a week for eight weeks. I remember crossing off each day on the calendar. During my radiation treatments I envisioned Jesus looking down at me and holding my hand. Then I remembered that old song: *["Jesus, Hold My Hand."* So every day while under the radiation machine I would sang the chorus to myself, it says: *"Blessed Jesus hold my hand I need thee every hour, thru this pilgrim land, protect me by thy power; Hear my feeble plea, O Lord, look down on me, When I kneel in prayer I hope to meet You there, Blessed Jesus hold my hand."]* It was difficult for me to talk for a while. Because of the tonsil surgery. (I had two-thirds of my tonsil removed and sixteen lymph nodes two of which were cancerous.) So, Larry answered the phone and talked to my friends. I got better every day and my goal was to sing again. For a while, I had a low gravelly voice. But again, God healed my voice and last year and this year I sang at the community center with our church choir. I am singing this Sunday at our new church location. Praise the Lord! My voice still does not have the range I used to have but God is faithful and I know it will eventually return.

I also had to have a feeding tube because I couldn't eat for a while. Finally, the time came for no more treatments but the feeding tube was in for several more months. Now the feeding tube is out and I am Cancer free. Hallelujah!

This is not the end of my story yet. Our friend Harry who I've mentioned before was staying with us while he was recovering from extreme skin cancer. He had surgery on his back and head. Harry was ninety-two and lived by himself so he stayed with us during this time. My precious husband was, caretaker, chief cook and bottle-washer for all of us.

One day we were walking into the kitchen to eat dinner and Larry was behind me he started to stumble and I tried to steady him and we both fell. Larry fell on top of me breaking my hip.

Got the picture? Our ninety-two-year-old friend hurried <u>as fast as he could</u>, and tried to help 82-year-old Larry and 81-year-old

Joyce get up. Though I was in pain it actually was funny. We called our son Trent he and our grandson Peyton came to our rescue. I had to go to the hospital and have a partial hip replacement. When the kids heard the whole story, they could not help but laugh and they said we would probably have won the Funniest Video on TV. But actually, they were very sympathetic and helpful. My husband tells people that he had a soft pillow to fall on so he was fine. God has healed my hip also.

I have knee problems and had planned on having knee surgery in fact had already made arrangements and had gotten the signature from my dentist which is required before knee surgery. Then I was diagnosed with cancer. Then I fell breaking my hip so I had to put it off.

Next Sunday I will be eighty-two, they do not want to do the knee surgery. When I fell, I skinned the left knee the one that always bothered me most. So now I'm asking God to heal my knees. Funny thing is, it seems with each need, to believe (without a doubt) like injured knees becomes a trial of my faith again. With all the miracles God has so graciously supplied in my life. You'd think I would have attained great faith by now. But I am still working on developing just the "mustard seed" faith. (Mathew 17:19)

I am still using the walker when I go places but I walk around the house without it.

I know that *"With God all things are possible"* Mathew 19:26b (KJV)

Joyce (Grammer) Lacey

Chapter 12

Princess Bride "Forever After"

One Day my Prince (Jesus) will come.

I want to end my memoir by thanking Jesus, the true "Prince." He has so graciously favored me with a joy and enthusiasm for life and especially for the life to come.

One Day, *Prince Jesus will come,* actually *riding on a white horse!* (Revelation 19:11) Then, in the same way that all fairy tales end, I will go with my *"*Prince*"* to His beautiful, majestic, home in heaven to live as His "Princess-Bride," *happily, ever after!*

Jesus said... *"I go to prepare a place for you; I will come again and receive you unto Myself; that where I am, there you may be also."* (John 14:3) [NAS]

All who receive Jesus have this promise. (John 3:16)

Ever wonder why fairy tales are so popular? Why magic is so alluring? Every human heart deeply desires to be rescued by someone wonderful and trustworthy. After endeavoring to overcome evil in life, our hope is that some day a "Prince" will come to guarantee that the future will be safe and secure forever after.

Fairy tales express that overwhelming desire. Therefore, though we think of them as fantasy, they actually tell the truth about God's majesty and victorious plan of good over evil. I recently came to the realization that God not only put eternity in our hearts (Ecclesiastes 3:11-12), but has made all peoples seek out the following scenario:

1) Good to overcome evil.

2) Someone powerful to come and rescue them.

3) To take them to a beautiful, perfect, and safe place.

4) To live "Happily Ever After"

I believe God, through the inspiration of the Holy Spirit, made me aware of why fairy tales are and have been so popular throughout all ages. We think they are just too good to be true. However, they are exactly what God lined out as His perfect plan for mankind. Notice the similarities of the two:

> In **Fairy tales**, *we see a witch or other things depicting evil,* **[The devil]** *doing it's best to destroy an innocent young "princess-bride."* **[The church]**

> **Fairy tale**: *Evil almost succeeds.* **[Our life on earth]**

> **Fairy tale**: *The "prince" comes charging in on a white horse to rescue the princess.* **[Jesus comes actually *riding on* a *white horse to rescue us*]**

> **Fairy tale**: *The prince then takes the princess as his bride to live with him in a Beautiful Palace.*

98

[Jesus comes and takes us, His Bride (the Church) to live with Him in His Majestic home in heaven] *(Eventually, the New Heaven and New Earth)*

Fairy tale: *The prince and princess live happily ever after.* **[We, His bride will   go to live with our Prince, King Jesus, to live, "Happily Ever After."]**

This thread runs through the entire story of my life as God would want it to in everyone's life story. Sadly, not everyone will choose to go with our Prince. Our kind and gentle Prince Jesus will never force Himself on anyone. They must choose to follow Him.

The following scriptures are so very encouraging in expressing our promised, "Happily, Ever After" that I want to leave these thoughts with you: [Parenthesis Mine]

> *"Then I saw a new heaven and a new earth, for the first heaven and the first earth had passed away, and there was no longer any sea. I saw the Holy City the New Jerusalem, (The Church) coming down out of heaven from God, prepared as a bride beautifully dressed for her husband. And I heard a loud voice from the throne saying,* **'Now the dwelling of God is with men, and He will be with them. They will be his people and God Himself will be with them and be their God. He will wipe every tear from their eyes. There will be no more death or mourning or crying or pain, for the old order of things has passed away'** *He who was seated on the throne said, 'I am making everything new' then He said, 'Write this down, for these words are trustworthy*

and true'. He said to me, 'It is done. I am the Alpha and the Omega, the beginning and the end" (Revelation 21: 1-6) NIV.

Revelation 21:9 "... *Come I will show you the bride* (the church) *the wife of the Lamb, and He carried me away in the Spirit to a mountain great and high, and showed me the Holy City, Jerusalem, coming down out of heaven from God." (NIV)*

How great is our God! What a great plan:

He will dwell with us and we will live with Him, *happily ever after*.

So dear reader did you solve the mystery???

Clue: Birthed by God, to give us a true _____ _____ (type) life now and forever after.

Pictures:

Our 50th Wedding Anniversary Celebration

August 26th 2007
On the Icon Yacht
Newport Beach. CA

A Gift from our Children

Joyce (Grammer) Lacey

Larry and Joyce on our 50th Wedding Anniversary

Todd and His Girlfriend Cindy

Joyce (Grammer) Lacey

Our Daughter and Family

Shane, Jill, Mick and Preston Mitchell

Our Son and Family

Trent, Jackie, Peyton and Vivian Lacey

Larry and Me with our Grandchildren
(Left to Right)
Preston, Peyton, Vivian and Shane

Our Grand-daughter Vivian Lacey
(Flower Girl)

Junior Flower Girls
(My niece: Gracie and Larry's niece: Kayla)

Renewing Our Vows (Don Hinkle Minister)

Introducing Larry and Me, (vows renewed)

Larry and Me (Joyce) at our 50th Anniversary Reception
August 26, 2007

Joyce (Grammer) Lacey

Our Beautiful Anniversary Cake
(Gold Shells were made of White Chocolate)

Family Picture
with Joyce's Niece Patti Jo
(Todd, Jill, Patti Jo, Joyce, Larry and Trent)

Professional TV Gospel Singer, Vern Jackson and Wife, Sandra
(Sandra and I have been friends since sixth grade)

From Little Pauper Girl to "Princess-Bride" For Ever After

Lightning Source UK Ltd.
Milton Keynes UK
UKHW021527120920
369688UK00001B/2/J